Testifying in Court

Testifying in Court

An Officer's Guide for Becoming a Better Witness

John Cagle

BOOKLOGIX®
Alpharetta, Georgia

Although the author has made every reasonable effort to ensure that the information in this book is correct, the author does not assume and hereby disclaims any liability to any party for any loss, damage, or disruption caused by errors or omissions, whether such errors or omissions result from negligence, accident, or any other cause.

ISBN: 978-1-6653-1160-1

This ISBN is the property of BookLogix for the express purpose of sales and distribution of this title. The content of this book is the property of the copyright holder only. BookLogix does not hold any ownership of the content of this book and is not liable in any way for the materials contained within. The views and opinions expressed in this book are the property of the Author/Copyright holder, and do not necessarily reflect those of BookLogix.

Printed in the United States of America

∞This paper meets the requirements of ANSI/NISO Z39.48-1992 (Permanence of Paper)

012826

"A good witness can't fix a bad case, but a bad witness can destroy a good one."

—John Cagle

Contents

Introduction		*ix*
Chapter One	*Arrest Warrants*	1
Chapter Two	*Preparing to Testify*	3
Chapter Three	*Common Pitfalls and How to Avoid Them*	9
Chapter Four	*Preliminary Hearings*	13
Chapter Five	*Bond Hearing*	15
Chapter Six	*Grand Jury*	17
Chapter Seven	*Pretrial Hearings*	19
Chapter Eight	*Pretrial Conference*	25
Chapter Nine	The Trial—*Jury Selection*	29
Chapter Ten	The Trial—*Opening Statements*	33
Chapter Eleven	The Trial—*The State's Case*	35
Chapter Twelve	The Trial—*The Defense*	43
Chapter Thirteen	The Trial—*Closing Arguments*	45
Chapter Fourteen	The Trial—*Judge's Charge to the Jury*	47
Chapter Fifteen	The Trial—*Jury Deliberations*	51
Chapter Sixteen	The Reward	53

Instructor Resources 55

Glossary 57

Acknowledgments 61

Introduction

Law enforcement officers have enormous powers, but we also have chances to exercise discretion. A phrase I often use is, "Just because we can, doesn't always mean we should."

Let me share this story: Just after turning sixteen, a young boy left his house, headed to church one afternoon, and about a mile away, he came upon a license checkpoint. As he reached for his wallet, he realized he had left his driver's license on his table at home.

When he approached one of the officers, he explained the situation. The officer could have easily issued a ticket, but instead, he exercised his judgment and told the boy to go back home, grab his wallet, and return. He told him not to be scared, and as he came back, the officer waved him through.

The boy learned a valuable lesson that day and will never forget his driver's license again.

This experience shows that just because we can do something doesn't mean we always should. The officer made a greater impact by exercising that judgment.

When law enforcement officers graduate from the basic academy, they sometimes do not understand the scope of their duties. Some older officers have forgotten them. We all should remember that we represent the citizens and the jurisdictions in which we work.

Criminal indictments read something like this:

> The State of ________, by and through the citizens of ________ County, charge and accuse ________ with the offense of ________.

Most citizens want us to succeed. We truly become the voice of victims—children who have been abused, elderly folks who have been abandoned, or a young mother killed by a drunk driver. Hard work in the field breeds success, but we can't stop there. Following through with our commitment also means representing them in court by adequately preparing for and presenting the facts through testimony. It's our duty to see it through and win.

Being a good witness goes beyond just showing up. Well-prepared witnesses are appreciated by judges, lawyers on both sides, and the ultimate decision makers: the jury.

Fear of the unknown causes stress in any setting, and the courtroom is no exception. But once you figure out what's going on, some of that stress will go away. The information in this guide is intended to explain some of the stages a criminal case goes through as it travels through the judicial process, and how to prepare to testify if you are called as a witness.

Chapter One

Arrest Warrants

In most jurisdictions, the process of applying for an arrest warrant is conducted remotely, making it more efficient. This nonconfrontational process involves a magistrate judge and is carried out via video chat most of the time.

Officers complete a standardized template provided by the court system to ensure all necessary details are included. Before issuing the warrant, the magistrate judge administers an oath to the officer, which is the first instance of this formal procedure in the judicial process.

The officers provide testimony as to the facts of the case. The magistrate will then determine if there is probable cause to issue a warrant.

Remember, probable cause is the threshold that must be met before a judge can issue a warrant. Probable cause means "more likely than not." Most of the time, that's a tiny hill to climb.

Convicting someone at trial can be a steep climb, however, because the threshold is beyond a reasonable doubt. The definition of reasonable doubt is simple: It is the doubt of a reasonable person seeking the truth. When considering the charges to apply for, you should be very confident in your climbing ability!

Chapter Two

Preparing to Testify

One of the most crucial aspects of being an effective witness is preparation. First and foremost, officers should review not only the reports they personally prepared, but also any reports from other officers involved in the case. Additionally, a review of body-camera footage and audio/video footage of suspect interviews is necessary. This ensures that you have a complete understanding of every detail of the incident.

A great way to prepare is to take notes from these reports as you get ready for testimony. While you may anticipate certain questions, if you're new to testifying, it's not always easy to predict everything. The key is to answer questions directly and succinctly, without adding opinions unless specifically asked.

It's also advisable to avoid taking the original reports to the witness stand. Instead, have a notebook with an outline of key points to refresh your memory if needed. Judges generally prefer that you speak from your knowledge rather than reading verbatim.

Remember that preliminary hearings are often early in the process, so the prosecutor might not have all the details. In that case, you may be asked to explain everything from the beginning without a lot of specific questions.

If you're not familiar with the configuration of the courtroom, take a look. Find the witness stand and have a seat. You will find that it's uncomfortable for many reasons. However, remember that the person occupying that seat is the most powerful in the room. Everyone is focused on each word spoken. Physical evidence is admitted through witnesses sitting in that chair.

After being called as a witness, you will approach the witness chair and keep standing until you are administered the oath. Then, have a seat and prepare for the first prompt from the prosecutor, which will always be "State your name and where you work."

So far, so good!

Then, more specific questions will come. These questions can go into more detail than you provided the judge when you applied for the arrest warrant. Since you studied the file, this stage should be a breeze. The prosecutor will stop asking questions when they believe they have met the threshold for probable cause.

As the defense lawyer stands to ask their questions, you will feel your heart rate increase a bit. Their goal is to convince the judge that there is not sufficient information to establish probable cause for the arrest. Their fallback goal is to find out about every aspect of the case.

In other words, how bad is it for their client?

The more time you spend in the courtroom, you will

learn that some lawyers are more aggressive than others. Don't let this bother you. Calmly answer the questions and let the prosecutor object when things get out of hand. Some defense lawyers might try to contact you before court to see if you will discuss the facts of the case. Don't! One aggressive lawyer I once knew would try to take the officers to lunch before court. If this happens to you, it might be a good time to cut back.

Your demeanor in the courtroom can significantly impact how your testimony is received. Here are some key points to keep in mind:

1. **Dress appropriately.** Your appearance should reflect the seriousness of the event. Whether in uniform or business attire, ensure that you are neat, clean, and professional.

2. **Mind your body language.** Sit up straight, make eye contact, and avoid fidgeting. These simple actions convey confidence and credibility. Often, the witness chair will swivel or rock; the jury will completely lose focus on the words spoken if a witness is moving around in the witness chair.

3. **Be courteous and respectful.** Address the judge as "Your Honor," and be polite to everyone in the courtroom, including the attorneys and court staff.

4. **Stay composed.** Court proceedings can sometimes be stressful, but maintaining your composure is crucial. Some defense lawyers will ask questions in an attempt to attack you both professionally and personally. Don't buy into that. It's an effort to make you mad and

distract the attention away from their client. Sometimes they will ask a question that requires a yes or no answer and quickly move on to another question.

Example:

> Question: "Did you see my client's face at the scene?"
>
> Answer: "No." (But the judge will allow you to explain your answer, e.g., "No, but the officer who chased him from the scene pulled his mask off, and I saw his face then.")

Defense lawyers don't want the jury to hear that part.

5. **Speak clearly and slowly.** This ensures that everyone can understand you and that your testimony is accurately recorded.

Law enforcement is a career filled with jargon that most folks don't understand. Don't use jargon in reports or when you are testifying. Answer questions with words everyone can understand.

A drug agent was testifying about searching a house for methamphetamine. He testified he found a pound of "ice," a slang term for meth, in the freezer. The grandmother on the jury looked up as if to say, "Isn't that where it's supposed to be?"

6. **Make Eye contact.** If it's a jury trial and you are asked to tell the jury about certain facts, look at them and answer the question. Make eye contact with a few jurors as you go. If a juror makes eye contact with you and responds positively, such as shaking their head in

agreement, it's a sign that they understand where you're going. This will always calm you down. Once you've answered that question, look back at the prosecutor and get ready for the next question. Unless you are told to "tell the jury," there is no need to look at them.

Chapter Three

Common Pitfalls and How to Avoid Them

Testifying in court usually is not difficult. Talking to the prosecutor beforehand, reviewing case reports and recordings, and practicing answering questions as you prepare will help you feel more at ease. Anyone who has had a speech class will remember the time spent speaking in front of a mirror, practicing the speech they must give during class. Once you realize the purpose of some questions, it will also get easier.

However, testifying in court is not something you will do that often; therefore, it's easy to become complacent. Remembering these common pitfalls will help you refocus on preparing to testify.

1. **Over-complicating your answers:** Keep your answers straightforward and to the point. Avoid unnecessary details that could confuse the listener.

2. **Inconsistency with reports:** Always ensure that your testimony matches the reports you've submitted. Discrepancies can weaken your credibility.

3. **Being unprepared for cross-examination:** The defense attorney may ask challenging questions. Stay calm and remember that it's okay to say you don't know something. But remember, there is a difference between "I don't know" and "I don't recall." "I don't know" means you never knew. "I don't recall" means that at one time you did know, but have forgotten.

4. **Allowing emotions to take over:** Court can be emotional, but it's important to remain composed and professional at all times.

5. **Neglecting to review all relevant information:** Make sure you're familiar with every detail of the case, not just your own involvement. This helps you answer questions more effectively.

6. **Stick to your guns:** Defense lawyers often try to offer a witness an alternative answer to a question answered previously.

Example:

There was a case where a car was broken into in the parking lot of a grocery store one afternoon. An elderly man was walking to his car and saw the suspect breaking into a vehicle. He was later able to identify the person in a photographic lineup. At trial, the elderly man, who was in his eighties, appeared in his usual attire: overalls. He took the witness stand, and when asked by the prosecutor if the person he saw that day was in the courtroom, he quickly identified the defendant.

The defense lawyer began to suggest to the old man that he had made a mistake and kept asking if there was any chance at all that he might be mistaken or in doubt of the identification. He insinuated that due to the man's age and potentially impaired eyesight, he couldn't make an identification. But the old man stuck to his guns and never wavered.

Growing frustrated, the defense lawyer finally asked the old man, "Just how far can you see?"

The old man thought for a moment and said, "Well, at night I can see the moon."

The jurors smiled and looked at the defense lawyer, as if wanting to say, "Take that." The lawyer slowly sat down. The jury convicted the defendant.

Chapter Four

Preliminary Hearings

Before the preliminary hearing, it's important to remember that you will be testifying in open court. This means the public and sometimes even family members of the defendant can be present.

For patrol officers, there's often a lot of gear to carry, such as a gun, a taser, handcuffs, extra magazines, a radio, and a bulletproof vest. All of this equipment might make it difficult to sit comfortably in the witness chair. Therefore, it's a good idea if your agency allows you to remove some of that gear and leave it secured in your car or at the courthouse. This can help you feel more at ease and focused while you're testifying.

The preliminary hearing is a step in the judicial process designed to confirm that there was probable cause to issue the arrest warrant and move the case forward. This hearing often occurs before the same magistrate judge who issued the warrant. It is the first adversarial hearing in the process.

The defendant will be present with their lawyer. The rules of evidence are slightly more relaxed than at a trial, allowing hearsay evidence, meaning witnesses can testify to what others may have said.

The main witness will be the officer who applied for the warrant. The prosecutor will ask the officer to explain the circumstances of the arrest, and then the defense attorney will cross-examine. While the primary purpose is to confirm probable cause, defense attorneys often try to explore every detail of the case, and most judges will give them some latitude in doing so.

Chapter Five

Bond Hearing

Often, bond hearings are held in conjunction with a preliminary hearing. The purpose of a bond hearing is to determine whether the defendant should be released on bond or if the State has valid reasons to object. Remember, a denial of bond is reserved for the most serious cases.

For the State to object to a bond, they must show cause that the defendant is either likely to flee the jurisdiction if released or is a danger to the community and may re-offend.

To prepare for a bond hearing, you should be ready to discuss the defendant's criminal history. This means conducting a criminal history check beforehand to know if the defendant has any prior offenses or convictions. If the defendant has a history of violence or has tampered with evidence, you should be prepared to testify to those details. If there were any threats made by the defendant toward witnesses or victims, you should be ready to detail those, as well. Remember that hearsay is admissible in this hearing.

Chapter Six

Grand Jury

In most states, following an arrest for certain criminal offenses, the State is required to present the case to a grand jury. The grand jury is comprised of citizens from the county where the offense happened. For federal offenses, grand jurors come from a geographic area where elements of the crime occurred.

The hearing is usually nonconfrontational. Typically, you are the sole witness, and the prosecutor will guide you through the details of the arrest and investigation.

Once reviewing the case, the prosecutor may sometimes add additional charges to the indictment that you may not be aware of. That's why it's important to review the indictment before your testimony, which will help avoid being taken off guard in the grand-jury room.

Hearsay is admissible during grand-jury proceedings. And occasionally, grand jurors may have their own questions.

Therefore, you must be prepared to answer any questions they ask.

For more complex or very serious cases, it can be beneficial to prepare charts or a brief presentation to help the grand jurors understand the facts more clearly and serve as a cheat sheet for you during your testimony. This material must be provided to the prosecutor well in advance and approved for use by them.

This testimony is important because the grand jury needs to be convinced that there is probable cause for the arrest and that the case should proceed to trial. It is a great opportunity for you to showcase your professionalism and knowledge, and practice your testimony skills in this relaxed setting.

It's also worth noting that in some states, grand-jury proceedings are not recorded by a court reporter, but are kept confidential. In federal court, all grand-jury proceedings are taken down by a court reporter.

Chapter Seven

Pretrial Hearings

As a case progresses and approaches trial, several legal matters must be addressed that require a hearing before the judge (no jury yet)—things such as motions (a request) to suppress evidence seized during searches or statements made by defendants. Officers involved in those matters will be the witnesses.

Preparing for these hearings is no different than preparing for any other proceeding. Review reports and audio/video footage, and meet with the prosecutor to prepare.

Search warrants are often used in certain investigations to search for and recover evidence of crimes. Affidavits for those warrants must contain certain critical information that establishes probable cause that evidence of the crime is located at a specific location. Preparing these documents is a skill set that requires officers to undergo specific training and be up to date with case law.

Often, evidence recovered during searches can be very damaging to defendants. This is the reason defense lawyers will fight so hard to exclude any evidence found. Developing this skill set can be both interesting and fun if done correctly.

If you are the affiant of a search warrant application, you will be the witness at this hearing. The defense lawyer will suggest that the warrant did not provide the judge with sufficient probable cause to issue the warrant. You will be subject to questioning about everything you provided the judge that is contained in the search warrant documents and any oral testimony given. For instance, if in the affidavit you stated that some information was provided to you by a reliable informant, you will likely provide details about the informant's past reliability—without, of course, giving names.

If you are a patrol officer, you will need to be familiar with and have a good working understanding of legal requirements that will allow you to search vehicles without first obtaining a search warrant. Exactly what happened during the traffic stop that gave you probable cause to search following the traffic stop?

For instance, as the driver was getting out of the car, you saw them drop a plastic bag of what, based on your training and experience, you believed was cocaine. You might be asked what training you've received and if you have seized something before that turned out to be cocaine. Or perhaps you conducted a field test on the sample, and it was positive for cocaine. Circumstances like this could allow you to search a vehicle without a warrant.

Another common vehicle search done during traffic stops is an inventory search. If the circumstances of the stop require that the vehicle be impounded, a search can be conducted to document any valuables inside. The search is not done to locate evidence of a crime. However, if evidence of a crime is found during this search, it can be seized and used in court.

Defense lawyers will try to get you to admit that the reason for the search was to locate evidence of crimes, instead of valuables. Don't fall for that. Remember, inventory searches should be conducted prior to the vehicle being impounded or without delay. A reason to delay the search might be safety reasons. However, searching a vehicle days after it was impounded requires a search warrant. Now, during an inventory search, you are not allowed to dismantle components of the vehicle to look for valuables.

You will be asked about the reason for the stop to confirm the stop was legal, and then the reason the vehicle was going to be impounded, i.e., the driver was arrested.

You will be asked if your agency has an impound policy that requires you to impound the vehicle. (It's a good idea to provide a copy of the policy to the prosecutor before this hearing and to have a copy with you on the witness stand.) You will probably be handed a copy of it by the prosecutor and asked to identify it.

Another common search is done incident to or immediately following an arrest—meaning when you arrest someone, you are allowed to search them (their pockets, clothing, and other belongings) for weapons. If you come upon evidence of a crime, you may seize it and use it in court. The key point allowing this search is the validity of the arrest or detention. Be prepared to discuss the factors that caused the arrest.

Consent searches are another exception to the warrant requirement. Under certain circumstances, individuals may permit officers to search homes, cars, suitcases, or other areas where they would otherwise expect privacy. Consent forms are used to document these searches, as well as audio/video recordings.

During a motion-to-suppress hearing, the officer obtaining consent will be the witness and should review the document and recordings of the consent. Defense lawyers will suggest that the consent was invalid because promises or threats were used during the process. Hopefully, your professional demeanor captured on your body-cam recordings proves them wrong.

Statements made by the defendant are helpful. That's also why defense lawyers fight very hard to exclude anything their client might have said. I've always said if they are talking, it's a good thing. If they are in custody, certain legal requirements are triggered.

In custody, questioning must be preceded by the defendant's advisement of Miranda rights. Before digital recorders and body cameras, the proof we advised someone of their Miranda rights came in the form of a document signed by the officers and the defendants. Back then, defense lawyers would imply that even if their client signed the document, they did so because they were promised something or threatened. Nowadays, most agencies still use the forms, but the advisement is audio/video recorded, thus removing the argument of promises or threats.

The hearing addressing the admissibility of statements, called a Jackson Denno hearing, is held before trial. It's a simple hearing for the purpose of establishing that the defendant was advised of Miranda rights, understood them, and knowingly waived those rights without any promises or threats made to them.

In preparation for this hearing, officers should review documents signed by the defendant and any audio/video recordings. Also, be prepared to recite verbatim the Miranda rights. It's a good habit when you advise someone of their rights in the field, refer to the form or the Miranda card you were issued. During the hearing and at trial, you will be asked what you read to the defendant, so have the card or form ready. One of the most embarrassing situations I've seen in court was an officer digging to reach his wallet through all his gear and searching through credit cards until he finally found the Miranda card. Painful!

These hearings are a chance to practice your testimony, because at trial, you will have to do it all over again.

Of course, there could be many other pre-trial legal matters to settle without the need for a witness.

Chapter Eight

Pretrial Conference

Let's review the steps that have been taken to put you in this position.

After considering all aspects of potential criminal charges, you apply your judgment and discretion and choose the most appropriate charges. In other words, the ones that you feel good about the chances of a conviction if there were a trial later. You overcame those "load 'em up" with silly knee-jerk charges and appeared before the judge to apply for warrants. There were preliminary hearings and bond hearings that gave you a chance to prepare for your testimony. During cross-examination, you learned some valuable lessons but prevailed. The grand jury went well and gave you another opportunity to practice your testifying skills. Several pretrial hearings gave you other chances to practice.

Now, the case is set for trial.

As the trial date approaches, the prosecutor will meet with all potential witnesses and provide them with an idea of what to expect during the trial, specifically their testimony. For instance, if you interview someone during the initial event, they will need to review the report of their interview to refresh their memory about what they saw or said. This is important because it has likely been some time since the crime occurred—sometimes years.

Remember, during discovery, the defense is supplied with the entire investigative file. That's the reason that all witnesses must review applicable reports and documents to ensure that no discrepancies occur during their testimony.

If you are the lead law-enforcement officer on the case, the prosecutor might ask you to participate in these pretrial conferences, and I encourage you to do that. It will serve as a great way for you to refresh your memory about things you may not have directly participated in, but you need to know about.

There will likely be other officers who will testify and will need your help to prepare. You must insist that they are ready. Offer them suggestions, such as a look at the courtroom and the witness stand. Just because the officer may be experienced and has been in the agency a long time, it doesn't mean they have testified a lot, if at all.

In some trials, several "lay witnesses" (non–law enforcement) may be called to testify. Most of them will have zero knowledge about trials and will be extremely nervous about testifying. Help them prepare, as you do with officers, and remind them that being a good witness is about telling the truth. The prosecutors will go into detail with them about their testimony, and you should be in a support role.

Most prosecutors' offices have investigators whose job

it is to assist in preparing for trial. If they are good, they will do a lot of heavy lifting, and you can learn from them.

Occasionally, there will be codefendants who, after reaching an agreement with the prosecutor, are called as witnesses during trial. Some will look at you as being the cause of their current predicament; therefore, it's usually a good idea to evaluate your role in their pretrial conference.

After the pretrial conferences are completed, the prosecutors will decide in what order the witnesses will testify. Think about it like an organized production or a play; each witness has a part in the play. It is choreographed in a way that enhances the jury's ability to follow along and understand it. So, think about pretrial conferences as a dress rehearsal for trial.

Chapter Nine
The Trial

Jury Selection

All criminal defendants are entitled to a jury trial by their peers in the jurisdiction where the offense took place. Selecting qualified jurors is important to both sides and can be a lengthy process. If you are the prosecuting officer, you might be asked to assist the prosecutor during jury selection. I encourage you to do that.

There are three stages of this process:

1. Courts will select potential qualified jurors from public records, such as voter registration lists. These individuals will receive a summons in the mail to appear in court on a day certain to continue the process. Along with the summons will be a juror questionnaire consisting of background questions, which will help the court and lawyers during the next phase of jury selection.

Some circumstances can disqualify someone from jury service. In some states, people above a certain age can be excused from jury duty. Non-US citizens can't serve on a jury, and convicted felons who have not regained their civil rights can't serve. Those convicted of traffic and misdemeanor offenses are allowed to serve.

2. On the day jurors are required to appear, they will be organized in groups called "panels." The judge will usually meet with the group and provide them with information about the importance of jury service. Some courts might show a short video stressing the duty of citizens to serve on a jury. Most judges will then ask a series of preliminary general questions of the panels to ensure everyone meets the minimum qualifications to serve as a juror on a particular case.

Then, individual panels are brought into the courtroom and asked more specific background questions by the court and the lawyers on both sides. That's where the questionnaires come in handy. During this phase, some jurors may be excused by the court for various reasons. Some reasons might include a health issue that could prevent them from sitting for long periods of time, or impaired hearing, which prevents them from hearing the witnesses. Other reasons, such as prior knowledge of the case, might prevent them from being impartial, or personal relationships with witnesses on either side could cause them to be excused. This entire process is called "voir dire" and is aimed at determining if a potential juror can be completely impartial during the trial.

3. The last phase of jury selection is the actual selection process. The lawyers from both sides will be given time by the judge to review any notes taken while questioning the jurors. During this review, the lawyers will attempt to dismiss or "strike" certain individuals they believe may not be beneficial to their side. In most states, both sides are given an equal number of strikes. However, in some cases, judges can increase the number of strikes for both sides. For felony cases, twelve jurors will be selected. For misdemeanor cases, six jurors are chosen.

In trials, there is a need to select "alternate," or additional, jurors. Jurors chosen as alternates will hear the case as usual, and if another juror is excused during the trial, one of the alternates will fill in.

Once all phases of jury selection have been completed, the jurors will be seated in the jury box, administered an oath by the judge, and given additional instructions.

Chapter Ten
The Trial

Opening Statements

Before they begin, the judge will instruct the jury that what the lawyers say during opening statements is not evidence.

During jury selection, the lawyers introduced themselves to the jurors, and during opening statements, they will do a little more of that. However, the purpose of an opening statement is to provide jurors with a roadmap of how they anticipate the trial will move forward.

The State/government has the burden to prove each element of the crimes charged in the indictment beyond a reasonable doubt. During the State's opening statement, they will briefly provide the jury with a preview of how they intend to do it. Since today's jurors often appreciate the use of technology and forensic science—such as fingerprints, DNA analysis, or cell-phone tracking—if the

State's case includes any of these, jurors will be alerted to watch for them during the trial. They will also be told to watch for other very damning evidence, such as eyewitness identifications and important physical evidence that will be presented.

At the conclusion of the State's opening statements, the lawyers will most always end it by saying, "After you've heard the evidence presented by the State, we will ask you to return a verdict of guilty of all counts in the indictment."

The defense lawyer will then present their version of what the jury can expect during the trial. They will always remind the jury that the State must prove its case beyond a reasonable doubt, and their client is not required to do anything. If the State's case doesn't include all that interesting forensic evidence or other evidence identifying the defendant, the defense lawyer will mention that during their opening statement.

Occasionally, a defense attorney will waive their opening statements. This usually means they really haven't decided what their defense is going to be.

Chapter Eleven
The Trial

The State's Case

Before a witness is called, the lawyers will ask the judge to invoke the Rule of Sequestration. This means that any witness in the courtroom must leave and is prohibited from discussing their testimony with another witness. If you are the prosecuting law enforcement witness, the prosecutor will likely ask the judge to allow you to remain at the prosecution table and assist during the trial. Since the burden of proof rests with the State, they will go first.

Remember, the prosecutor has determined what witnesses will be called and in what order they will testify. This is where all those pretrial conferences come into play, and if the witnesses are prepared.

You should listen carefully to all the testimony and take notes. The prosecutor will have an outline of the topics to be covered with each witness, but sometimes you may pick up on something they haven't covered. Glances at the jurors can help you spot confused faces during witness testimony.

Once everything is covered with the State's witness, the defense will ask its own questions. This is called cross-examination. Their questions are intended to challenge the information given during the State's questions. Once the defense is through, the State will call its next witness, and this process will continue during the trial.

There are several ways evidence is presented during a trial. Direct evidence is the testimony of a person who asserts that they have actual knowledge of a fact, such as an eyewitness identification of a suspect or the recovery of a certain piece of physical evidence. Circumstantial evidence is proof of a set of facts and circumstances that tend to prove or disprove another fact by reference.

Here is an example of circumstantial evidence. My eight-year-old granddaughter asked if she could have a grape drink in the refrigerator. As I'm leaving the room, I tell her no, but I will pour her a glass of milk after I come back from the mailbox. When I return, I see that the grape drink is missing from the refrigerator, and the empty bottle is in the trash can. I look at her and notice that she has grape-colored stains around her lips. I didn't see her drink it, but I can consider all the circumstances to conclude she did.

Testimonial evidence is the answers given by witnesses as they testify. Other pieces of physical evidence may be admitted during a trial (guns, photographs, scientific evidence, including blood or fingerprints found at a scene). These exhibits must be introduced during witness testimony. This requires testimony about the integrity of the evidence; where it was obtained and by whom must be established. There are legal requirements for the admission of evidence, and it is the job of both sides to adhere to those requirements.

The prosecuting law enforcement officer will play an important role during the presentation of both testimonial and physical evidence. It's not uncommon for the prosecution to attempt to admit most of the physical evidence through law enforcement, which could prolong the testimony. The need to prepare for this process is utmost. The better job done during the collection of evidence and the proper handling of it afterward can make this easier. Remember, this is usually the most critical portion of the trial and one that is most frequently attacked by the defense.

There are certain questions witnesses will be asked as evidence is attempted to be admitted. If you are this witness, you would have heard them already during the pretrial conference. You should have examined each exhibit you are going to identify during your testimony.

Depending on the type of case, photographs can be important for the jury to see, and there could be many. While on the witness stand, you will be handed these photographs, which have already been marked by the prosecutor with exhibit numbers, and asked if you can identify them. Remember, you have seen them before, so quickly scan through them. Your answer should be "yes."

Then, you will be asked how you can identify them. Your answer might be that these are the photographs of the inside of the house at 123 Green Street on the evening of the incident.

Then, you will be asked if they are true and accurate representations of how you found the house on the night of the incident. Your answer should be "yes." Note: If you did not actually take the pictures but were present as they were being taken, you can testify to them.

Following this series of questions, the prosecutor will ask the judge to admit those exhibits. Once admitted by the judge, you will be asked to tell the jury what each picture depicts. This is usually done by projecting them using an overhead projector. This procedure will be followed until all the photographs have been displayed.

Admitting other pieces of physical evidence might require more attention. For instance, evidence that requires the tracking of its chain of custody—such as drugs, bodily fluids, guns, and other types that could be contaminated if mishandled—requires more specific testimony. A good job up front by properly marking and labeling this kind of evidence will make this go smoother.

Testifying about this kind of evidence might be like this: You will be handed the item and asked if you can identify it and how. If it was collected properly, it should have points of identification on it or the evidence bags it's stored in, such as your initials, date, and case number. The prosecutor will ask the judge to admit it as evidence. Once it is admitted, you will be asked to tell the jury where it was found and collected, and how the chain of custody was tracked. You will not be asked about any scientific tests performed on those items unless you are qualified to do so. Once they are admitted as evidence, you will move on to the next one.

After the evidence you can testify to has been admitted, you will be questioned about other aspects of the case you participated in. Even though you are aware of tasks performed by someone else or statements made to you by someone other than the defendant, you can't testify to it because it's hearsay.

Remember, in the preliminary hearings, hearsay was admissible, but not now.

Also, if the defendant made statements to you either before or after they were in custody, you may testify to those. The Jackson Denno hearing held earlier was the rehearsal for these questions. You will be asked to recite the Miranda rights you read to the defendant, so be prepared. If the defendant signed any Miranda waiver forms, you will be asked to identify those.

If there are any recordings of these interviews, the prosecutor will ask you about them and where they took place. You will be asked about the type of recorders used and if they were capable of adequately recording the conversations.

If a body camera was used, you will need to explain the audio delay in the beginning. You will be asked if you have reviewed the recordings and if they accurately reflect what was said during the interview. The prosecutor will ask the judge to admit them, and they will be played for the jury.

This process will repeat itself for all interviews of the defendant that the prosecutor wishes to present.

You may be privy to prior arrests or convictions the defendant may have had. You are not allowed to disclose that information during the trial. For instance, if the crime for which the defendant is currently on trial involved a firearm, and they were charged with illegally possessing it based on their prior convictions, and this trial is not addressing that charge, you must not mention those details. This information could call the defendant's character into question and likely cause a mistrial. The prosecutor will discuss this restriction during the pretrial conference.

Several tasks performed by law enforcement officers in the field require specialized training and advanced certifications. These might include:

- Accident reconstruction
- Radar operation
- Field sobriety testing
- Intoximeter operation
- Presumptive drug testing
- Explosive ordnance disposal (EOD)
- Canine and canine-handler detection activities
- Cellular-telephone data extraction and recovery actions
- Specialized electronic-surveillance activities
- FAA-approved drone operations

Witness testimony concerning these activities always includes a discussion of the required training for this skill set and the dates of the certification. If a recertification is required, the dates of the recertifications must be provided. During their testimony, officers may be required to produce copies of the actual certification documents to be introduced. If certain instruments or software were used, records of calibration and functionality will be presented.

Canine handlers should produce the canine-training certifications and training records. The breed of the canine and the language used to communicate with the canine, along with the alert indicators, will be presented in court. And, records of reliable alerts must be provided. Jurors enjoy watching and listening to canines in action, so be prepared.

I must continue to stress the importance of a thorough review of audio/video recordings of these events as reports are completed. Any discrepancies in the reports and recordings can cause irreparable damage to witness testimony.

There are some isolated exceptions to the disclosure of methods and operations of specialized enforcement actions.

These may include mitigation methods for explosive devices. The witness can testify that the object was made safe without disclosing how. Disclosing those methods could cause bomb makers to change the configuration of their devices to defeat mitigation methods used by bomb technicians.

Officers who wish to obtain these advanced skill sets and certifications will expend a lot of time and energy achieving them. Therefore, they should spend time preparing to showcase their skills in court.

After the prosecution has finished direct examination, it's time for the defense to cross-examine. Remember the suggested ways to answer questions and the need to explain answers if necessary. Just answer the questions directly without volunteering unnecessary details. Stay firm, and don't lose your temper. If you don't know the answer, say so, and don't fall into the speculation trap. If you hear the prosecutor object to a question, stop answering it and give time for the judge to rule on the objection. If the objection is sustained (agreed to) by the judge, you will not need to continue your answer.

Once the defense has finished its cross-examination, it is common for the prosecutor to have follow-up questions for clarification. This should be brief.

Once all witnesses have testified and the physical evidence has been admitted, the prosecutor will inform the judge that the State has concluded their presentation and rests.

It's now time for the defense to present its case.

Chapter Twelve
The Trial

The Defense

After the State has presented its case, it's time for the defense to respond.

Often, a motion will be made outside the presence of the jury, suggesting to the judge that the State has failed to meet its burden by proving its case beyond a reasonable doubt; therefore, the case should be dismissed. Defense lawyers will give their legal arguments, and the prosecutor will respond. Unless something has drastically gone wrong, the State usually prevails, and the judge will allow the jury to make the final determination. But, pay close attention to the defense arguments; there might be something in there you can use in future cases to improve something and remove their argument.

The defendant is not required to put forward any evidence or testify. But most of the time, some witnesses are called to challenge some of the State's witnesses. The decision to testify or not rests solely with the defendant. Lawyers often discourage it during certain types of cases, but can't stop them. If wishing to testify, the defendant will take an oath to tell the truth, like any other witness, and lawyers who ask questions soliciting answers they know to be lies can suffer severe penalties.

This is a moment during a trial when ethical decisions are important. I once had a trial when the defendant insisted on testifying to what could only be a lie. When presented with this dilemma, the defense lawyer asked him if he had anything he wished to tell the jury and sat down. No other questions were asked, and the defendant rambled on, telling one lie after another.

Fortunately, this was a good lawyer who made the correct ethical decision. Unfortunately, others don't.

Take notes during the defense's case presentation to help prosecutors cross-examine their witnesses. Watch the expressions on jurors' faces; you can often tell if they are buying the defense. I have always heard something during the defense case that I could use to improve during the next one. So, trial experience can offer a learning opportunity in many ways.

Once the defense has concluded its case, the State can offer rebuttal witnesses, if necessary. After that, the evidentiary phases of the trial are over.

Chapter Thirteen
The Trial

Closing Arguments

At the conclusion of the evidentiary phases of the trial, the lawyers for both sides have the chance to address the jury for the last time. In their opening remarks, they gave the jury an outline of what they expected to prove during the case. Now, they will remind the jury of some testimony and evidence that was admitted, which they believe supports their theory of the case.

Certainly, if there was scientific evidence tending to show the guilt of the defendant, the prosecutor would remind the jury. If there was a lack of scientific evidence, the defense would bring that up. If witnesses did a poor job during their testimony, that will most certainly be mentioned.

The judge will remind the jury that what the lawyers say in their closing arguments is not evidence.

Chapter Fourteen
The Trial

Judge's Charge to the Jury

At the conclusion of the closing statements by both sides, the judge will give the jury additional instructions regarding the law. These instructions are important to the jurors, but they can be very instructional to law enforcement officers.

Essentially, these instructions are the road map that jurors must follow during their deliberations of the case. But they also contain information that officers can consider and follow during the cases they investigate. In other words, knowing what's needed for a jury to convict a defendant can help during the collection of evidence in the field.

The following are excerpts from the pattern jury charges given by judges:

> "The defendant is presumed to be innocent until proven guilty. This presumption remains with the defendant until it is overcome by the State with evidence that is sufficient to convince you beyond a reasonable doubt that the defendant is guilty as charged. However, the State is not required to prove the guilt of the accused beyond all doubt or to a mathematical certainty. If the State fails to prove the defendant's guilt beyond a reasonable doubt, it would be your duty to acquit the defendant. But if that doubt does not exist in your minds as to the guilt of the accused, then you would be authorized to convict the defendant.
>
> "The jury must determine the credibility of the witnesses. In deciding this, you may consider all the facts and circumstances of the case, including the witness's manner of testifying, their means and opportunity of knowing the facts about which they testify, the nature of the facts about which they testify, the probability or improbability of their testimony, their interest or lack of interest in the outcome of the case, and their personal credibility as you observe it.
>
> "The defendant in a criminal case may take the stand and testify and be examined and cross-examined as any other witness. However, the defendant does not have to present evidence or testify. If the defendant chooses not to testify, you may not consider that in any way in making your decision."

The judge will instruct the jury regarding any statements made to officers following their arrest.

> "To be voluntary, a statement must be freely and willingly given without coercion, duress, threats, use of violence, fear of injury, or any suggestions or promises of leniency or reward. You must determine whether the defendant was advised of his/her constitutional rights and whether the defendant clearly understood and knowingly gave up such rights."

The judge will give the legal definition of the crimes alleged in the indictment and the elements that must be proven beyond a reasonable doubt for the jury to convict the defendant of those crimes, and any other legal definitions they are required to give. So, if the case has multiple counts in an indictment, this process will be lengthy. Listen closely as the judge describes each crime, consider the evidence that was admitted, and ask yourself, *Are we in good shape?*

Because that's what the jury is about to do.

Chapter Fifteen
The Trial

Jury Deliberations

After the instructions to the jury, the jurors will be told to go to the jury room and elect one of them as the foreperson who will preside over their deliberations. Once they receive the evidence that was admitted during the trial, they can begin to deliberate.

From time to time during deliberations, juries have questions they would like the judge to answer. They will send a note to the judge with the question. If it is something the judge is going to address, the jury will be brought back into the courtroom for further instructions by the judge. Sometimes the judge will not answer specific questions about evidence and will simply tell the jury they must rely on the testimony or evidence they heard presented from the witness stand. If it is a question that they can legally address, they usually will.

Depending on the nature of the case, jury deliberations can take from only a few minutes to several days. For me, waiting on a jury is difficult and often fosters a feeling of helplessness. Nothing can be done at this point but wait.

In a criminal case, to convict someone, the vote of the jury must be unanimous. If this is the case, the jury will send a message to the judge that they have reached a verdict and return to the courtroom.

It is at the discretion of the judge who will read the verdict. It could be the foreperson of the jury, the clerk of the court, or the judge.

Once the verdict has been read, the judge will have a few closing remarks to the jury, thanking them for their service, and they will then be dismissed.

Chapter Sixteen

The Reward

After all the hard work studying reports, prepping witnesses, identifying and marking exhibits, and sweating through jury deliberations, you finally hear the word you hoped for: "Guilty."

In federal cases, before the defendant is sentenced, a presentence report is completed, which helps the judge at sentencing. In state cases, a judge may order a presentence report or sentence the defendant directly after the verdict.

By going through each step in the judicial process, you have learned and become better. In your next case, you will remember the questions asked by the defense attorney and the look on the faces of the jury when they didn't understand your answer. You will most likely think to yourself, *I won't let that happen again*.

The instructions given to the jury by the judge will

resonate in your mind when you are making charging decisions in the future, and the words "beyond a reasonable doubt" will hopefully drive those decisions. And, most importantly, being successful at trial will give you confidence and strength for the next one.

Instructor Resources

This guidebook combines knowledge and best practices, allowing law enforcement officers to develop a clear understanding of the many judicial proceedings in criminal courts and how to prepare to be an effective witness. Basic law enforcement academies are required to teach a broad array of skills to cadets, and instruction time is a commodity. Every cadet can be provided with a copy of this guidebook to not only familiarize themselves with the content, but they can also refer to it as the need arises, when their court appearances increase.

Also, as an added benefit for instructors at academies and agencies, a detailed slide-deck presentation is provided along with recommended exam questions covering the material. They are available here:

https://drive.google.com/drive/folders/16ANsKG7tfveQCEJ9kAGrXIKdW3Dr9kC2?usp=sharing or request them from the author at testifyincourt@gmail.com.

Glossary

Acquittal
A judgment of not guilty for a person who has been charged with a crime.

Adversarial system
A criminal proceeding that pits one side against another.

Affidavit
A document confirmed by an oath.

Arraignment
A hearing during which a defendant in a criminal case pleads guilty or not guilty.

Burden of proof
An obligation of a party in a judicial proceeding to prove its position.

Case-in-chief
That portion of a judicial proceeding during which the party with the burden of proof presents evidence.

Case-in-rebuttal

That portion of a judicial proceeding in which a party can present rebuttal evidence challenging evidence given during a case-in-chief.

Crime

A violation of the law, punishable by a penalty of some form. More serious crimes are called felonies. Less serious crimes are called misdemeanors.

Cross examination

Questioning of a witness by the opposing side.

Defendant

The person accused of a crime.

Direct examination

The questioning of a witness by the side that has called them to testify.

Exhibit

A piece of evidence presented during a trial.

Hearing

A formal proceeding before a court.

Inadmissible

Objects, facts, or circumstances that cannot be presented in court.

Indictment

A formal charging document returned by a grand jury.

Judge

A person presiding over a criminal proceeding.

Juror

A person chosen to be on the jury.

Jury

The group of individuals selected to consider evidence presented during a trial.

Miranda rights

Certain rights that must be read to a suspect of a crime who is in custody at the time of questioning.

Mistrial

An invalid trial usually occuring if a serious mistake is made or a jury cannot reach a verdict.

Motions

A request made to a judge to decide an issue.

Objection

A disagreement regarding certain testimony or evidence.

Plea

When a defendant admits or denies a criminal accusation.

Plea bargain

A process during which parties agree on an outcome of a criminal case, thus preventing a trial.

Subpoena

A document demanding the presence of a witness or the production of certain documents.

Testimony

Statements made by witnesses during a criminal proceeding.

Trial

A formal proceeding in court where the facts of a case are presented.

Venue

The geographic location where criminal charges may take place.

Verdict

A decision made by a jury.

Witness

A person who is called to testify during a judicial proceeding.

Acknowledgments

I want to thank the following individuals for their suggestions and help with this guidebook:

Dr. Rebecca Caviness, Investigator, Appalachian Judicial Circuit

Chief Investigator Travis Greene, Appalachian Judicial Circuit

Other Books By John Cagle

Write to Protect and Serve:
An Officers Guide For Writing Better Police Reports

Those Days in January:
The Abduction and Murder of Meredith Hope Emerson

www.ingramcontent.com/pod-product-compliance
Lightning Source LLC
LaVergne TN
LVHW022314200926
848481LV00004B/1346